Cloud Kitchens Unveiled

A Comprehensive Guide to Launching and Scaling Your Culinary Empire

Raj Dev Acharya

FanatiXx Publication
www.fanatixxpublication.com

Raj Dev Acharya

FanatiXx Publication
D9, Seth Deokarandas Complex, Kachery Road, Rourkela
ISO 9001:2015 CERTIFIED
Website: www.fanatixxpublication.com

© **Copyright, 2022,** Raj Dev Acharya

All rights reserved. No part of this book may be reproduced, stored in a retrieval system, or transmitted, in any form by any means, electronic, mechanical, magnetic, optical, chemical, manual, photocopying, recording or otherwise, without prior written consent of the author.

Cloud Kitchens Unveiled
By: Raj Dev Acharya
ISBN: 978-93-5605-967-2
1st Edition

Price: 299.00 INR
Printed and Typeset by: BooksClub.in

The opinions/ contents expressed in this book are solely of the author and do not represent the opinions/ stands/ thoughts of FanatiXx.

DISCLAIMER

All rights reserved. This book may not be reproduced in whole or in part, or transmitted in any form, without written permission from the publisher, nor may any part of this book be reproduced, stored in a retrieval system, or transmitted in any form or by any means electronic, mechanical, photocopying, microfilming, and recording without written permission from the publisher.

Author assures that all content is original and he/she has full rights to publish and distribute the same. In any case of plagiarism, the publisher is not liable.

Contents

Introduction: The Culinary Frontier Unveiled 11
Chapter 1: The Evolution of Cloud Kitchens 17
Chapter 2: Crafting Your Unique Culinary Concept 27
Chapter 3: Setting Up Your Cloud Kitchen 35
Chapter 4: Embracing Technology for Efficiency 43
Chapter 5: Navigating Marketing in the Digital Age 51
Chapter 6: Creating a Stellar Brand 59
Chapter 7: Customer Retention Strategies 67
Chapter 8: Operational Excellence 75
Chapter 9: Financial Management 83
Chapter 10: Scaling Your Culinary Empire 91

Conclusion: Building and Sustaining a Thriving Cloud Kitchen 98
About the Author: 101
A Personal Invitation to Explore the World of Cloud Kitchens .. 105

Raj Dev Acharya

Raj Dev Acharyais not just an entrepreneur; he is a visionary leader with a rich tapestry of experience spanning over 30 years. His journey in the business world has been shaped by an unwavering passion for innovation, a commitment to personal growth, and an innate ability to navigate the complexities of the entrepreneurial landscape.

Introduction:

In an era where technology meets gastronomy, the rise of cloud kitchens has revolutionized the food industry. This book serves as your go-to manual, providing a step-by-step guide to help aspiring entrepreneurs set up, run, and thrive in the dynamic world of cloud kitchens. From the initial concept to scaling your culinary empire, we will explore every facet of this innovative business model.

Chapter 1: The Evolution of Cloud Kitchens
- Understanding the concept of cloud kitchens
- Tracing the historical evolution
- Exploring the market trends and opportunities

Chapter 2: Crafting Your Unique Culinary Concept
- Identifying your niche and target audience
- Menu development strategies for a virtual presence
- Leveraging data and market research for menu optimization

Chapter 3: Setting Up Your Cloud Kitchen
- Choosing the right location and infrastructure
- Designing an efficient kitchen layout
- Complying with regulations and safety standards

Chapter 4: Embracing Technology for Efficiency
- Implementing a robust order management system
- Integrating kitchen automation for streamlined operations
- Leveraging data analytics for decision-making

Chapter 5: Marketing in the Digital Age

- Building a compelling online presence
- Social media strategies for cloud kitchens
- Collaborating with food delivery platforms

Chapter 6: Creating a Stellar Brand
- Developing a unique brand identity
- Designing an eye-catching logo and packaging
- Building a cohesive brand narrative

Chapter 7: Customer Retention Strategies
- Implementing loyalty programs and discounts
- Gathering and analyzing customer feedback
- Personalizing the customer experience

Chapter 8: Operational Excellence
- Managing inventory and supply chain
- Staff training for efficiency and quality
- Implementing sustainable practices

Chapter 9: Financial Management
- Budgeting and forecasting for cloud kitchens
- Pricing strategies for profitability
- Managing costs and maximizing revenue

Chapter 10: Scaling Your Culinary Empire
- Replicating success in new locations
- Exploring franchise and partnership opportunities
- Be innovative and overcome competition

Conclusion:
"Cloud Kitchens Unveiled" is not just a book; it's your roadmap to success in the exciting world of virtual culinary ventures. Whether you're a seasoned entrepreneur or a

passionate food lover with a dream, this guide will equip you with the knowledge and strategies needed to turn your cloud kitchen into a thriving business. Get ready to embark on a journey where the fusion of technology and culinary artistry creates a recipe for unparalleled success.

Introduction: The Culinary Frontier Unveiled

Welcome to the gastronomic revolution of the 21st century, where the traditional boundaries of brick-and-mortar restaurants are dismantled, and the digital age meets the art of culinary creation. In the ever-evolving landscape of the food industry, a new protagonist has emerged: the cloud kitchen. This book, "Cloud Kitchens Unveiled," is your comprehensive guide to navigating this culinary frontier, from the inception of an idea to scaling a thriving empire.

The Genesis of a Culinary Shift

The concept of cloud kitchens has roots in the demand for convenience and the accelerating pace of modern life. As urban dwellers find themselves entwined in the hustle and bustle of daily existence, the demand for high-quality, on-demand food experiences has skyrocketed. Enter the cloud kitchen — an ingenious fusion of culinary artistry and technological prowess.

Our journey begins by dissecting the evolution of cloud kitchens. We explore the historical antecedents, tracing the footsteps of pioneers who dared to reimagine the restaurant experience. From the first virtual kitchens to the current state of the industry, we dissect the trends and opportunities that have shaped the culinary landscape.

Crafting Your Culinary Vision

A successful cloud kitchen starts with a compelling culinary concept. Chapter 2 delves into the intricacies of crafting a unique and resonant vision for your cloud kitchen. We discuss the importance of identifying your niche and understanding your target audience. From there, we guide you through the delicate art of menu development, exploring strategies that optimize not just taste but also profitability.

In a digital realm where the screen is your storefront, mastering the art of visual and culinary appeal is paramount. Leveraging data and market research, we unveil the strategies to ensure your menu not only satisfies the palate but resonates with the hearts and minds of your customers.

Setting the Foundation: Infrastructure and Location

As with any business venture, the foundation sets the tone for success. Chapter 3 is dedicated to the nitty-gritty of setting up your cloud kitchen. We dissect the critical decisions, from choosing the right location to designing an efficient kitchen layout. Moreover, we delve into the complexities of regulatory compliance and safety standards, ensuring that your culinary haven is not just a feast for the senses but a fortress of operational integrity.

Embracing Technology: The Heartbeat of Efficiency

At the heart of every successful cloud kitchen beats a robust technological infrastructure. Chapter 4 takes you on a journey through the tech-savvy side of the culinary world.

We explore the implementation of advanced order management systems, the integration of kitchen automation for streamlined operations, and the transformative power of data analytics in decision-making. Your cloud kitchen isn't just a place to cook; it's a symphony of algorithms and culinary mastery.

Marketing in the Digital Age

In a world where attention spans are shorter than ever, mastering the art of digital marketing is non-negotiable. Chapter 5 becomes your compass through the intricacies of building a compelling online presence. From social media strategies tailored to the virtual nature of cloud kitchens to collaborations with food delivery platforms, we illuminate the path to making your cloud kitchen a digital sensation.

Creating a Stellar Brand

A brand is more than just a name; it's an identity. Chapter 6 is a journey into the creation of a brand that transcends the digital realm. We discuss the development of a unique brand identity, the design of an eye-catching logo and packaging, and the construction of a cohesive brand narrative. In a world saturated with options, your brand is the beacon that guides customers to your culinary haven.

Customer Retention: Beyond the First Bite

The success of any culinary venture lies not just in acquiring customers but in retaining them. Chapter 7 is a deep dive into customer retention strategies, exploring the implementation of loyalty programs, the art of discounts, and the invaluable practice of gathering and analyzing customer feedback. In the digital age, personalization is the key to customer loyalty, and we show you the way.

Operational Excellence: Beyond the Kitchen

Efficiency isn't just confined to the kitchen; it permeates every facet of your cloud kitchen business. Chapter 8 is your guide to operational excellence, covering everything from inventory management and supply chain logistics to staff training for both efficiency and quality. Furthermore, we explore the implementation of sustainable practices, ensuring that your culinary success is not just profitable but also responsible.

Financial Management: Navigating the Bottom Line

The financial health of your cloud kitchen is the heartbeat of sustainability. Chapter 9 equips you with the tools to navigate the financial landscape, covering budgeting and forecasting, pricing strategies for profitability, and the delicate balance of managing costs while maximizing revenue. Your cloud kitchen is not just a culinary haven; it's a business, and understanding the financial intricacies is key to its longevity.

Scaling Your Culinary Empire

The journey doesn't end with the launch of your cloud kitchen; it's just the beginning. Chapter 10 explores the strategies for scaling your culinary empire. From replicating success in new locations to exploring franchise and partnership opportunities, we guide you through the nuances of staying innovative and ahead of the competition. Your cloud kitchen isn't just a local sensation; it's a global phenomenon in the making.

Conclusion: The Culinary Odyssey Awaits

"Cloud Kitchens Unveiled" is not just a book; it's your companion on a culinary odyssey. Whether you're a seasoned entrepreneur seeking to diversify or a passionate food lover with a dream, this guide is your roadmap to success in the exciting world of virtual culinary ventures. Get ready to embark on a journey where the fusion of technology and culinary artistry creates a recipe for unparalleled success. The culinary frontier awaits—let's unveil it together.

Chapter 1: The Evolution of Cloud Kitchens

Section 1: Understanding the Concept of Cloud Kitchens

In the labyrinth of culinary innovation, the emergence of cloud kitchens marks a paradigm shift in the traditional restaurant model. To embark on this journey, we first need to unravel the essence of cloud kitchens.

1.1 Defining Cloud Kitchens

At its core, a cloud kitchen is a virtual kitchen space that operates exclusively for fulfilling online orders. Unlike traditional restaurants, cloud kitchens lack a physical dining area, focusing solely on the production of delectable dishes to be delivered to customers' doorsteps. Understanding the intricacies of this concept is crucial for anyone venturing into the culinary world of the future.

1.1.1 The Virtual Culinary Realm

Delving into the virtual realm, cloud kitchens leverage the power of technology to bridge the gap between culinary craftsmanship and digital convenience. By embracing the online space, these kitchens redefine the dining experience, catering to the contemporary consumer's need for efficiency and quality.

1.1.2 The Diversity of Models

Cloud kitchens encompass various models, from single-brand virtual restaurants to multi-brand operations. Unraveling the nuances of these models is essential for prospective cloud kitchen entrepreneurs, as it informs critical decisions in crafting a unique culinary identity.

1.2 The Operational Dynamics

Beyond the absence of a physical dining space, cloud kitchens differentiate themselves through streamlined operations. The absence of in-house dining staff and the integration of advanced technologies create an operational efficiency that is central to their success.

1.2.1 Advanced Technology Integration

Cloud kitchens thrive on technology, employing state-of-the-art order management systems, kitchen automation, and data analytics. The orchestration of these elements transforms the kitchen into a finely tuned symphony of culinary precision and digital prowess.

1.2.2 A Culinary Laboratory

The absence of a dining area allows cloud kitchens to function as culinary laboratories, where chefs experiment with flavors, refine recipes, and optimize operations without the constraints of a traditional restaurant setting. This flexibility is a cornerstone of their evolution.

Section 2: Tracing the Historical Evolution

The roots of cloud kitchens stretch back further than one might imagine. Understanding their historical evolution unveils the journey from conceptual infancy to the booming industry we witness today.

2.1 Early Experiments

The concept of kitchens dedicated solely to fulfilling online orders has its seeds in the late 20th century. Early experiments, often driven by tech-savvy entrepreneurs and forward-thinking chefs, laid the groundwork for what would later become a culinary revolution.

2.1.1 Precursors to Cloud Kitchens

Examining the precursors to cloud kitchens reveals the gradual separation of cooking spaces from traditional dining establishments. Catering services and commissary kitchens foreshadowed the notion of kitchens operating independently from the traditional restaurant setting.

2.1.2 The Tech Boom Influence

The late 1990s and early 2000s witnessed a surge in technological advancements, setting the stage for the convergence of culinary arts and digital innovation. The rise of online platforms and food delivery apps catalyzed the separation of kitchens from dining spaces, giving birth to the first wave of cloud kitchens.

2.2 Pioneering Moments

The early 2010s mark a significant turning point in the evolution of cloud kitchens. Pioneering entrepreneurs and chefs, driven by a vision for culinary reinvention, began experimenting with virtual restaurants, paving the way for a new era in the food industry.

2.2.1 The Rise of Virtual Restaurants

The concept of virtual restaurants gained momentum as chefs recognized the potential to reach a broader audience without the constraints of physical location. These early ventures laid the groundwork for the diverse ecosystem of cloud kitchens we see today.

2.2.2 Technological Catalysts
Technological advancements, particularly in mobile connectivity and app development, acted as catalysts for the proliferation of cloud kitchens. The seamless integration of online ordering platforms and delivery services fueled the expansion of virtual culinary ventures.

Section 3: Exploring the Market Trends and Opportunities
To navigate the realm of cloud kitchens successfully, one must grasp the current market trends and seize the abundant opportunities it presents.

3.1 The Global Surge
The worldwide embrace of online food delivery and the growing demand for convenient dining options contribute to the global surge of cloud kitchens. Analyzing the geographical spread of this phenomenon unveils opportunities for entrepreneurs to tap into emerging markets.

3.1.1 Asian Markets: Pioneers in Adoption
Asian markets, particularly China and India, emerged as early adopters of cloud kitchens. Understanding the factors that fueled their rapid growth provides valuable insights for entrepreneurs eyeing international expansion.

3.1.2 The Western Wave
In the West, cloud kitchens gained prominence with the rise of food delivery platforms. Analyzing the market dynamics in

the United States and Europe reveals the nuanced trends that shape the industry in different cultural landscapes.

3.2 Consumer Preferences and Behavior
The success of a cloud kitchen hinges on its ability to align with evolving consumer preferences. Examining the shifting trends in dining behavior and culinary expectations provides a strategic advantage in crafting a menu that resonates with the target audience.

3.2.1 The Demand for Health-Conscious Options
As health consciousness grows, cloud kitchens are presented with opportunities to cater to the demand for nutritious and balanced meals. Exploring the intersection of culinary innovation and wellness trends unveils avenues for differentiation in a competitive market.

3.2.2 Customization and Personalization
The modern consumer craves personalized experiences. Cloud kitchens equipped with the tools to offer customizable menus and personalized recommendations stand at the forefront of culinary innovation.

3.3 The Role of Technology in Shaping the Future
Technological innovation continues to shape the trajectory of cloud kitchens. Understanding the evolving role of technology in enhancing customer experiences, optimizing operations, and expanding market reach is paramount for sustainable growth.

3.3.1 Artificial Intelligence and Predictive Analytics

The integration of artificial intelligence and predictive analytics empowers cloud kitchens to anticipate customer preferences, optimize inventory management, and enhance overall operational efficiency. Exploring the applications of these technologies unveils a future where kitchens operate with unparalleled foresight.

3.3.2 The Rise of Ghost Kitchens

The concept of ghost kitchens, detached from any specific brand and catering to multiple virtual restaurants, represents a trend with profound implications for the industry. Analyzing the opportunities and challenges associated with ghost kitchens provides a strategic lens for entrepreneurs.

Section 4: Challenges and Considerations

The evolution of cloud kitchens, while promising, is not without challenges. Acknowledging and understanding these challenges is crucial for entrepreneurs seeking to navigate this dynamic landscape.

4.1 Regulatory Complexities

Operating in the digital space doesn't exempt cloud kitchens from regulatory considerations. Understanding the legal landscape, including food safety regulations and licensing requirements, is imperative to avoid pitfalls that could jeopardize the success of a cloud kitchen.

4.1.1 Navigating Food Safety Standards

As with traditional restaurants, cloud kitchens must adhere to stringent food safety standards. Unraveling the intricacies of compliance ensures that the virtual culinary space maintains the trust and confidence of its customers.

4.2 The Logistics Conundrum
Efficient logistics are the backbone of cloud kitchen operations. Addressing the challenges associated with last-mile delivery, optimizing supply chain management, and mitigating issues related to food packaging are critical components of sustaining a successful cloud kitchen.

4.2.1 Last-Mile Delivery Innovations
In an era where delivery speed and reliability are paramount, exploring innovations in last-mile delivery, such as drone and autonomous vehicle technologies, offers a glimpse into the future of cloud kitchen logistics.

4.3 The Competitive Landscape
The proliferation of cloud kitchens has led to an increasingly competitive landscape. Entrepreneurs must navigate this space strategically, identifying opportunities for differentiation, collaboration, and innovation to stand out in a crowded market.

4.3.1 Branding and Differentiation
Crafting a unique brand identity is essential for cloud kitchens to carve a niche in the market. Analyzing successful branding strategies and differentiation tactics employed by industry leaders unveils the keys to standing out amidst the competition.

Section 5: Conclusion
As we conclude our exploration of the evolution of cloud kitchens, one thing becomes clear: we stand at the intersection of tradition and innovation, where culinary artistry meets digital convenience. Understanding the

concept, tracing its historical evolution, and exploring market trends and opportunities are foundational steps in the journey toward building and scaling a successful cloud kitchen.

In the subsequent chapters, we will delve deeper into the practical aspects of setting up and running a cloud kitchen. From crafting a unique culinary concept to embracing technology, marketing strategies, and customer retention, this guide is designed to equip you with the knowledge and insights needed to thrive in the dynamic realm of cloud kitchens. So, buckle up as we embark on a culinary adventure where the evolution of cloud kitchens becomes the backdrop for your entrepreneurial success.

Cloud Kitchens Unveiled

Chapter 2: Crafting Your Unique Culinary Concept

Section 1: Evaluating Your Niche and Target Audience

In the vast landscape of culinary creativity, the first step towards building a successful cloud kitchen is identifying a niche that aligns with your passion and resonates with a specific target audience. This section delves into the intricacies of discovering your culinary niche and understanding the nuances of your target audience.

1.1 Understanding the Power of Niche

1.1.1 Defining Your Culinary Identity

Crafting a unique culinary concept begins with a clear definition of your identity. What makes your offerings stand out in a crowded market? Unraveling the essence of your culinary identity is crucial for establishing a foundation that resonates with your target audience.

1.1.2 Niche as a Competitive Advantage

Exploring the concept of niche markets as a competitive advantage sheds light on how narrowing your focus can lead to a more profound impact. We dissect successful examples of cloud kitchens that have mastered the art of niche targeting.

1.2 Mapping Your Target Audience

1.2.1 Profiling Your Ideal Customer
Identifying your target audience involves creating detailed customer personas. We explore methodologies for constructing accurate and actionable customer profiles, considering factors such as demographics, psychographics, and behaviors.

1.2.2 Analyzing Market Segmentation
Delving into market segmentation, we dissect how dividing the market into specific segments allows for more targeted marketing efforts. Understanding the varied preferences within your target audience is key to tailoring your culinary concept effectively.

1.2.3 The Importance of Localization
Acknowledging the influence of local tastes and cultural preferences, we discuss the significance of adapting your culinary concept to the specificities of the geographic areas you serve. Localization is a powerful tool for resonating with diverse audiences.

Section 2: Menu Development Strategies for a Virtual Presence
With a clear understanding of your niche and target audience, the next phase of crafting a compelling culinary concept involves developing a menu that not only tantalizes taste buds but also translates well in the virtual space. This section explores the intricacies of menu development strategies tailored for a cloud kitchen.

2.1 The Art of Virtual Presentation

2.1.1 Visual Appeal in the Digital Realm
Understanding the impact of visual appeal in the online space, we delve into the art of presenting your menu virtually. From high-quality food photography to intuitive design, we explore strategies to make your offerings visually enticing.

2.1.2 Storytelling Through Menus
Crafting a menu is not just about listing dishes; it's about telling a story. We discuss the art of menu storytelling, where each dish contributes to the narrative of your culinary concept. A well-crafted menu elevates the required customer experience.

2.2 Flexibility and Customization

2.2.1 Embracing Adaptability
The dynamic nature of the culinary industry calls for a menu that can adapt to changing trends and customer preferences. We explore the concept of flexibility in menu development, allowing your cloud kitchen to evolve without losing its core identity.

2.2.2 The Power of Customization
Analyzing the demand for personalized dining experiences, we discuss the strategic incorporation of customization options in your menu. From build-your-own dishes to tailored flavor profiles, customization enhances customer satisfaction and loyalty.

2.3 Strategic Pricing and Profitability

2.3.1 Setting the Right Price Point

Determining the optimal price point for your menu involves a delicate balance between affordability and profitability. We explore pricing strategies that align with your brand positioning while ensuring financial sustainability.

2.3.2 Maximizing Profitability Through Menu Engineering

Menu engineering is a science that combines psychology and economics. We dissect the principles of menu engineering, including the strategic placement of high-margin items and the removal of underperforming dishes, to maximize overall profitability.

Section 3: Leveraging Data and Market Research for Menu Optimization

The digital age has ushered in an era where data and market research play a pivotal role in shaping business strategies. In this section, we explore how cloud kitchens can leverage data analytics and market research to optimize their menus for maximum impact.

3.1 The Role of Data in Culinary Decision-Making

3.1.1 Harnessing Data for Insights

We delve into the ways cloud kitchens can harness data to gain actionable insights into customer preferences, popular menu items, and operational efficiency. From order history to customer feedback, data becomes a valuable tool in crafting a menu that resonates with your audience.

3.1.2 Predictive Analytics for Menu Forecasting

The integration of predictive analytics allows cloud kitchens to forecast demand, optimize inventory levels, and minimize waste. We explore how forecasting tools can be employed to make informed decisions regarding menu items, ensuring that you consistently meet customer demand without excess inventory.

3.2 Customer Feedback and Iterative Improvement

3.2.1 The Importance of Customer Feedback

Understanding the significance of customer feedback, we discuss strategies for collecting and analyzing input from your audience. Customer feedback becomes a valuable resource for identifying areas of improvement, refining recipes, and staying attuned to changing preferences.

3.2.2 Iterative Menu Optimization

Embracing a mindset of continuous improvement, we explore the concept of iterative menu optimization. By using data and customer feedback, cloud kitchens can iteratively refine their menu, ensuring that it remains dynamic and responsive to evolving culinary trends.

3.3 Competitor Analysis for Strategic Positioning

3.3.1 Identifying Competitor Strengths and Weaknesses

A comprehensive competitor analysis provides insights into the strengths and weaknesses of other players in the market. We guide cloud kitchen entrepreneurs in conducting a thorough analysis, allowing them to position their menu strategically and capitalize on unmet customer needs.

3.3.2 Differentiation Through Innovation

Examining case studies of successful cloud kitchens, we highlight how innovation can be a powerful tool for differentiation. Whether through unique menu items, novel culinary techniques, or creative presentation, innovation becomes a driving force in capturing market attention.

Section 4: Conclusion

Crafting a unique culinary concept for a cloud kitchen is an art that combines passion, market understanding, and data-driven decision-making. By identifying your niche, understanding your target audience, developing a visually appealing and flexible menu, and leveraging data and market research, you lay the foundation for a culinary concept that not only survives but thrives in the dynamic and competitive landscape of cloud kitchens.

In the subsequent chapters, we will delve deeper into the practical aspects of setting up and running a cloud kitchen. From embracing technology and efficient kitchen operations to marketing strategies, customer retention, and brand building, this guide is designed to equip you with the knowledge and insights needed to turn your culinary vision into a thriving reality. So, let the aroma of innovation guide you as you embark on the culinary journey of crafting your unique cloud kitchen concept.

Cloud Kitchens Unveiled

Chapter 3: Setting Up Your Cloud Kitchen

Section 1: Choosing the Right Location and Infrastructure

The success of a cloud kitchen is intricately tied to its physical foundation. In this section, we delve into the critical decisions surrounding location and infrastructure, exploring how these choices impact efficiency, accessibility, and overall operational success.

1.1 The Significance of Location

1.1.1 Understanding the Target Audience Geography

The choice of location should align with the demographics and preferences of your target audience. We explore the importance of understanding the geographic distribution of your customer base and how it influences decisions about where to establish your cloud kitchen.

1.1.2 Accessibility and Delivery Radius

Analyzing the accessibility of potential locations, we discuss the importance of optimizing the delivery radius. Proximity to key delivery routes and densely populated areas is crucial for timely and efficient order fulfillment.

1.1.3 Navigating Urban Dynamics

For cloud kitchens operating in urban environments, we explore the unique dynamics of city settings. From considerations of traffic patterns to leveraging data on population density, urban location decisions are nuanced and strategic.

1.2 Infrastructure Requirements

1.2.1 Adequate Space for Operations
Selecting a location that provides sufficient space for kitchen operations is fundamental. We discuss the spatial requirements for equipment, storage, and a seamless workflow to avoid bottlenecks in the cooking and delivery process.

1.2.2 Tech-Ready Infrastructure
The integration of technology is at the core of cloud kitchen operations. We explore the infrastructure requirements for a tech-ready kitchen, including considerations for high-speed internet, order management systems, and connectivity with delivery platforms.

1.2.3 Scalability in Infrastructure
Anticipating future growth is essential when setting up the initial infrastructure. We delve into scalable solutions that allow your cloud kitchen to expand seamlessly, accommodating increased order volumes and the potential addition of new culinary concepts.

Section 2: Designing an Efficient Kitchen Layout
Efficiency is the heartbeat of a successful cloud kitchen. In this section, we dissect the principles of designing an efficient kitchen layout, ensuring that every square foot is optimized for productivity and culinary excellence.

2.1 Ergonomics in Kitchen Design

2.1.1 Workflow Optimization
Efficient workflow is the foundation of kitchen design. We explore strategies for organizing kitchen stations to minimize movement, reduce preparation time, and enhance overall productivity.

2.1.2 Ergonomic Considerations for Staff
Prioritizing the comfort and safety of kitchen staff is paramount. We discuss ergonomic design principles, including the arrangement of workstations, the placement of equipment, and the consideration of factors like lighting and ventilation.

2.2 Equipment Selection and Placement

2.2.1 Identifying Essential Equipment
Choosing the right equipment is a pivotal decision. We provide a comprehensive guide to identifying the essential kitchen appliances and tools for your cloud kitchen, considering factors such as menu complexity and anticipated order volume.

2.2.2 Optimal Equipment Placement
Efficient kitchen layout goes hand in hand with strategic equipment placement. We explore best practices for arranging cooking stations, prep areas, and storage units to minimize bottlenecks and maximize efficiency.

2.3 Kitchen Safety and Hygiene

2.3.1 Adherence to Safety Standards
Safety in the kitchen is non-negotiable. We discuss the importance of adhering to safety standards, including fire safety protocols, proper ventilation, and the use of appropriate materials in the kitchen space.

2.3.2 Hygiene Practices and Sanitation
Maintaining impeccable hygiene is a cornerstone of cloud kitchen operations. We explore best practices for sanitation, from regular cleaning routines to staff training on food safety protocols.

2.4 Technology Integration for Operational Excellence

2.4.1 Order Management Systems
Integrating a robust order management system is critical for streamlined operations. We discuss the functionalities of these systems, from order processing to inventory management and analytics.

2.4.2 Kitchen Automation Tools
Automation tools contribute to efficiency by minimizing manual tasks. We explore the role of kitchen automation, from smart appliances to automated order routing, in enhancing overall productivity.

Section 3: Complying with Regulations and Safety Standards

Navigating the regulatory landscape is a crucial aspect of establishing a cloud kitchen. This section provides a comprehensive guide to complying with regulations and safety standards, ensuring legal integrity and the well-being of both customers and staff.

3.1 Licensing Requirements

3.1.1 Understanding Local Licensing Regulations
Licensing requirements vary across regions. We guide entrepreneurs through the process of understanding and obtaining the necessary licenses for operating a cloud kitchen in their specific location.

3.1.2 Food Handling and Safety Certifications
Compliance with food safety regulations is paramount. We explore the certifications and training programs necessary for kitchen staff to handle food safely and maintain hygiene standards.

3.2 Health and Safety Protocols

3.2.1 Developing a Health and Safety Manual
Creating a comprehensive health and safety manual is a proactive approach to compliance. We guide entrepreneurs through the process of developing a manual that outlines protocols for both staff and kitchen operations.

3.2.2 Employee Training on Safety Protocols
Ensuring that all staff members are trained on safety protocols is essential. We discuss strategies for conducting

regular training sessions, emphasizing the importance of ongoing education in maintaining a safe work environment.

3.3 Environmental and Sustainability Compliance

3.3.1 Waste Management Practices

Sustainable waste management practices are increasingly important. We explore strategies for minimizing kitchen waste, recycling, and incorporating environmentally friendly practices in day-to-day operations.

3.3.2 Energy Efficiency Measures

Reducing the environmental impact of a cloud kitchen involves adopting energy-efficient measures. We discuss the implementation of energy-saving technologies, from LED lighting to energy-efficient appliances.

Section 4: Conclusion

Setting up a cloud kitchen requires meticulous planning and a keen understanding of the interplay between location, infrastructure, kitchen layout, and regulatory compliance. By choosing the right location, designing an efficient kitchen layout, and ensuring compliance with regulations and safety standards, you lay the groundwork for a cloud kitchen that not only meets but exceeds operational expectations.

In the following chapters, we will explore additional aspects of cloud kitchen management, from embracing technology and effective marketing strategies to ensuring customer satisfaction and building a strong brand. So, as you embark on the journey of setting up your cloud kitchen, let the principles outlined in this chapter guide you toward a foundation of excellence and success.

Chapter 4: Embracing Technology for Efficiency

In the fast-paced world of cloud kitchens, technology is the driving force behind operational efficiency. This chapter delves deep into the implementation of technology solutions to optimize every aspect of your cloud kitchen, from order processing to kitchen operations and data-driven decision-making.

Section 1: Implementing a Robust Order Management System

An efficient order management system is the backbone of a successful cloud kitchen. In this section, we explore the intricacies of implementing a robust system that ensures seamless order processing, accurate inventory management, and enhanced customer satisfaction.

1.1 Understanding the Role of Order Management

1.1.1 The Central Nervous System of Cloud Kitchens

An order management system (OMS) serves as the central nervous system, coordinating various functions within a cloud kitchen. We dissect the critical role an OMS plays in orchestrating the flow of orders from the point of entry to fulfillment.

1.1.2 Real-Time Order Tracking and Communication

The integration of real-time order tracking enhances customer experience and facilitates effective communication between the kitchen and delivery partners. We explore the features that contribute to the transparency and efficiency of order tracking.

1.2 Selecting the Right Order Management System

1.2.1 Tailoring OMS to Business Needs

Cloud kitchens come in various shapes and sizes, each with unique operational requirements. We discuss the importance of selecting an OMS that aligns with the specific needs of your cloud kitchen, considering factors such as menu complexity, order volume, and integration capabilities.

1.2.2 Scalability and Future-Proofing

Anticipating growth is essential when choosing an OMS. We explore considerations for scalability, ensuring that the system can accommodate an increase in order volume and additional features as your cloud kitchen expands.

Section 2: Integrating Kitchen Automation for Streamlined Operations

Efficiency in kitchen operations is paramount for a cloud kitchen's success. In this section, we delve into the world of kitchen automation, exploring how technology can streamline processes, reduce errors, and enhance overall productivity.

2.1 The Role of Kitchen Automation

2.1.1 Enhancing Accuracy and Consistency

Kitchen automation minimizes human error, ensuring that each dish is prepared with precision and consistency. We discuss the impact of automation on the quality of food and customer satisfaction.

2.1.2 Streamlining Workflow for Speed
Efficient workflow is the key to timely order fulfillment. We explore how kitchen automation tools, from automated cooking appliances to smart prep stations, contribute to speeding up operations without compromising quality.

2.2 Automated Inventory Management

2.2.1 Preventing Stockouts and Wastage
Automated inventory management systems play a crucial role in preventing stockouts and minimizing wastage. We discuss how these systems track ingredient levels in real-time, enabling proactive ordering and reducing unnecessary costs.

2.2.2 Integration with Suppliers for Seamless Replenishment
The integration of inventory systems with suppliers streamlines the replenishment process. We explore the benefits of automated communication with suppliers, ensuring that ingredients are restocked efficiently to meet demand.

2.3 Smart Appliances and IoT in the Kitchen

2.3.1 Improving Efficiency with Smart Appliances

Smart appliances equipped with Internet of Things (IoT) technology revolutionize the kitchen environment. We delve into how these devices, from connected ovens to intelligent food processors, contribute to operational efficiency.

2.3.2 Data-Driven Insights from IoT Devices

IoT devices generate valuable data that can inform decision-making. We explore how cloud kitchens can leverage insights from connected appliances to optimize recipes, monitor equipment performance, and enhance overall efficiency.

Section 3: Leveraging Data Analytics for Decision-Making

In the data-driven landscape of cloud kitchens, leveraging analytics is essential for making informed decisions. This section explores how data analytics can be harnessed to optimize menu offerings, enhance customer experiences, and drive overall business success.

3.1 The Power of Data in Cloud Kitchens

3.1.1 Transforming Data into Actionable Insights

Data analytics transforms raw data into actionable insights, guiding strategic decision-making. We discuss the types of data relevant to cloud kitchens and how to extract meaningful information from it.

3.1.2 Analytics for Menu Optimization

Data-driven menu optimization involves analyzing customer preferences, popular dishes, and sales trends. We explore how cloud kitchens can use analytics to refine their menus, introduce new offerings, and enhance overall profitability.

3.2 Customer Insights and Personalization

3.2.1 Understanding Customer Behavior
Analyzing customer data provides valuable insights into behavior patterns. We discuss the importance of understanding customer preferences, order history, and feedback to personalize the customer experience.

3.2.2 Tailoring Marketing Strategies with Analytics
Data analytics informs targeted marketing strategies. We explore how cloud kitchens can leverage customer insights to tailor promotional campaigns, discounts, and loyalty programs for maximum impact.

3.3 Operational Efficiency Through Analytics

3.3.1 Optimizing Kitchen Operations
Data analytics plays a crucial role in optimizing kitchen operations. We discuss how cloud kitchens can use data to identify bottlenecks, streamline workflows, and improve overall operational efficiency.

3.3.2 Predictive Analytics for Demand Forecasting
Predictive analytics enables cloud kitchens to forecast demand accurately. We explore how forecasting tools can be used to anticipate order volumes, optimize inventory levels, and enhance overall planning.

Section 4: Ensuring Data Security and Compliance

With the increasing reliance on technology and data, ensuring the security and compliance of sensitive information is paramount. This section explores strategies for safeguarding data, complying with regulations, and building trust with customers.

4.1 Data Security Best Practices

4.1.1 Implementing Secure Data Storage

Cloud kitchens must prioritize secure storage of customer and operational data. We explore best practices for implementing encryption, access controls, and other measures to protect sensitive information.

4.1.2 Employee Training on Data Security

Human error is a common vulnerability. We discuss the importance of employee training programs to educate staff on data security best practices and cultivate a culture of cyber hygiene.

4.2 Regulatory Compliance in the Digital Age

4.2.1 Navigating Data Protection Laws

Data protection laws vary globally. We guide cloud kitchens in navigating regulations such as GDPR, HIPAA, and others, ensuring compliance with regional and industry-specific data protection standards.

4.2.2 Transparency in Data Handling

Building trust with customers involves transparency in data handling. We explore communication strategies for informing customers about data practices, privacy policies, and security measures.

Section 5: Conclusion

Embracing technology for efficiency in a cloud kitchen is a multifaceted endeavor that involves the strategic implementation of order management systems, kitchen automation, and data analytics. By optimizing the technological backbone of your cloud kitchen, you not only streamline operations but also gain valuable insights for informed decision-making.

In the subsequent chapters, we will further explore essential aspects of cloud kitchen management, from effective marketing strategies and customer retention to building a strong brand and ensuring culinary excellence. As you navigate the technological landscape of your cloud kitchen, let the principles outlined in this chapter guide you toward a future where innovation and efficiency go hand in hand.

Chapter 5: Navigating Marketing in the Digital Age

In the contemporary culinary landscape, the advent of cloud kitchens has revolutionized the way food is prepared, ordered, and delivered. With this shift comes the imperative need to navigate the complexities of marketing in the digital age. This chapter serves as a comprehensive guide to understanding and executing effective digital marketing strategies for cloud kitchens, covering the nuances of building a compelling online presence, leveraging social media platforms, and strategically collaborating with food delivery services.

Section 1: Building a Compelling Online Presence

Establishing a robust online presence is the cornerstone of successful digital marketing for cloud kitchens. Your online presence encompasses various elements, including your website, social media profiles, and digital content. Each component plays a critical role in shaping your brand identity and attracting customers. Let's delve into each aspect and explore best practices for optimization:

1.1 Website Optimization:
Your website serves as the virtual storefront for your cloud kitchen. It ought to possess visual allure, user-friendliness, and optimization for desktop and mobile interfaces alike.
- ✓ Incorporate high-quality images of your menu items to entice visitors and stimulate their appetite.

- ✓ Ensure easy navigation and seamless functionality, including intuitive menu browsing, online ordering capabilities, and secure payment processing.
- ✓ Integrate search engine optimization techniques to accelerate your website's visibility and improve its ranking on search engine results pages.
- ✓ Consider including customer testimonials, reviews, and ratings to build credibility and trust.
- ✓ Social Media Integration:
- ✓ Social media platforms offer unparalleled opportunities for engaging with your target audience and amplifying your brand's reach.
- ✓ Create and maintain active profiles on relevant platforms such as Instagram, Facebook, Twitter, and TikTok.
- ✓ Develop a cohesive content strategy that showcases your culinary creations, behind-the-scenes glimpses, promotions, and special events.
- ✓ Encourage user-generated content by sharing customer photos and reviews, fostering a sense of community around your brand.
- ✓ Utilize social media advertising features to target specific demographics, promote offers, and drive conversions.

1.2 Content Creation:

- ✓ Engaging content is essential for captivating and retaining your audience's interest.
- ✓ Experiment with different types of content, including videos, blog posts, infographics, and interactive polls.
- ✓ Share stories and anecdotes that humanize your brand and resonate with your audience on a personal level.

- ✓ Consistently publish fresh and relevant content to keep your audience engaged and encourage repeat visits to your website and social media profiles.
- ✓ Monitor analytics data to track the performance of your content and identify opportunities for optimization and improvement.

Section 2. Social Media Strategies for Cloud Kitchens

Social media has become a dominant force in the digital marketing landscape, offering unparalleled opportunities for connecting with consumers and driving engagement. For cloud kitchens, leveraging social media effectively is essential for building brand awareness, fostering customer loyalty, and driving sales. Let's explore some strategies for harnessing the power of social media:

2.1 Platform Selection:
- ✓ Choose social media platforms that align with your target audience and brand objectives.
- ✓ Instagram is ideal for visually showcasing your menu items and behind-the-scenes content.
- ✓ Facebook provides a platform for community building, customer engagement, and targeted advertising.
- ✓ Twitter can be used for real-time updates, promotions, and customer service interactions.
- ✓ TikTok offers a creative outlet for showcasing your culinary skills and personality through short-form videos.

2.2 Content Strategy:

- ✓ Create a content schedule delineating the kinds of content you intend to share and their scheduled release times.
- ✓ Balance promotional posts with engaging and entertaining content to maintain audience interest.
- ✓ Experiment with different content formats, such as images, videos, stories, and polls, to keep your feed dynamic and diverse.
- ✓ Encourage user-generated content by reposting customer photos and reviews and featuring them on your social media profiles.
- ✓ Track engagement metrics like likes, comments, shares, and follower counts to assess the impact of your social media endeavors.

2.3 Community Engagement:
- ✓ Proactively interact with your audience, ensuring timely responses to comments, messages, and mentions.
- ✓ Encourage community building by initiating discussions, posing inquiries, and actively seeking feedback from your followers.
- ✓ Collaborate with influencers, food bloggers, and other brands to expand your reach and tap into new audiences.
- ✓ Leverage user-generated content by reposting and sharing customer photos and testimonials, thereby encouraging brand advocacy and loyalty.

Section 3: Collaborating with Food Delivery Platforms

In the era of convenience-driven dining, partnering with food delivery platforms is essential for reaching customers beyond your physical location and increasing your sales potential. However, navigating the landscape of food delivery services requires careful consideration and strategic planning. Let's explore the key aspects of collaborating with food delivery platforms:

3.1 Platform Selection:
- ✓ Evaluate the various food delivery platforms available in your area and choose those that align with your target audience and business objectives.
- ✓ Consider factors such as commission fees, delivery radius, customer base, and platform reputation when making your selection.
- ✓ Explore partnerships with multiple platforms to maximize your reach and diversify your revenue streams.

3.2 Menu Optimization:
- ✓ Adapt your menu offerings to suit the unique demands of online ordering and delivery.
- ✓ Prioritize items that travel well and maintain their quality during transit, such as soups, salads, sandwiches, and bowls.
- ✓ Streamline your menu to simplify the ordering process and minimize delivery times.
- ✓ Clearly communicate any special instructions, dietary restrictions, or allergen information to ensure a positive customer experience.

3.3 Operational Efficiency:
- ✓ Implement systems and processes to manage incoming orders efficiently and ensure timely delivery.

- ✓ Integrate your point-of-sale (POS) system with food delivery platforms to streamline order fulfillment and minimize errors.
- ✓ Train your staff to handle online orders effectively and provide excellent customer service throughout the delivery process.
- ✓ Monitor order volumes, delivery times, and customer feedback to identify areas for improvement and optimization.

3.4 Marketing and Promotion:
- ✓ Leverage the marketing resources and promotional opportunities offered by food delivery platforms to increase your visibility and attract new customers.
- ✓ Offer exclusive deals, discounts, and promotions to incentivize customers to order through the platform.
- ✓ Collaborate with the platform's marketing team to feature your cloud kitchen in promotional campaigns, newsletters, and social media posts.
- ✓ Encourage satisfied customers to leave positive reviews and ratings on the platform, which can enhance your visibility and reputation.

Section 4: Conclusion

Marketing in the digital age presents both challenges and opportunities for cloud kitchens seeking to establish a competitive edge in the culinary market. By building a compelling online presence, leveraging social media effectively, and strategically collaborating with food delivery platforms, cloud kitchens can attract new customers, foster customer loyalty, and drive sales growth. It's essential to approach digital marketing with a strategic mindset, continually monitoring and optimizing your efforts to adapt to evolving consumer preferences and market trends. With the strategies outlined in this chapter, you'll be well-equipped to navigate the complexities of marketing in the digital age and position your cloud kitchen for long-term success and profitability.

Chapter 6: Creating a Stellar Brand

In the competitive world of cloud kitchens, a strong and distinctive brand is the key to standing out and building lasting connections with customers. This chapter explores the process of creating a stellar brand, covering everything from developing a unique identity to crafting a compelling narrative.

Section 1: Developing a Unique Brand Identity

A brand's identity is its personality, and in the culinary world, it's the flavor that sets it apart. This section delves into the intricacies of developing a unique brand identity for your cloud kitchen.

1.1 Defining Your Brand Personality

1.1.1 Core Values and Mission

Your brand's core values and mission form the foundation of its personality. We explore strategies for defining these elements, ensuring they align with your culinary vision and resonate with your target audience.

1.1.2 Differentiation in a Saturated Market

In a market saturated with culinary options, differentiation is crucial. We discuss techniques for identifying unique selling propositions (USPs) that set your cloud kitchen apart and create a distinctive brand identity.

1.2 Target Audience Alignment

1.2.1 Understanding Audience Preferences
A successful brand resonates with its audience. We explore methods for understanding the preferences, lifestyles, and aspirations of your target audience, enabling you to tailor your brand to their tastes.

1.2.2 Adapting to Changing Consumer Trends
Consumer trends evolve, and so should your brand. We discuss the importance of staying attuned to changing preferences, allowing your brand to adapt and remain relevant in a dynamic market.

1.3 Visual Elements of Branding

1.3.1 Color Psychology in Branding
Colors evoke emotions and associations. We explore the psychology of colors in branding, guiding you in selecting a color palette that aligns with your brand personality and creates the desired emotional connection with customers.

1.3.2 Typography and Visual Consistency
Consistency in visual elements is paramount. We delve into the role of typography in conveying your brand's tone and personality, and the importance of maintaining visual coherence across all brand materials.

1.4 Brand Naming Strategies

1.4.1 Reflecting Culinary Identity in the Name
Your brand name is a crucial element of your identity. We explore strategies for choosing a name that reflects your

culinary identity, is memorable, and resonates with your target audience.

1.4.2 Checking Trademarks and Domain Availability

Practical considerations, such as trademark availability and domain name availability, are essential in the naming process. We guide you through the steps of conducting thorough checks to avoid legal issues and secure a unique brand name.

Section 2: Designing an Eye-Catching Logo and Packaging

Visual elements, such as logos and packaging, play a significant role in brand recall and customer perception. This section explores the design principles and strategies for creating an eye-catching logo and packaging for your cloud kitchen.

2.1 Designing a Memorable Logo

2.1.1 Simplicity and Versatility

A memorable logo is simple and versatile. We discuss the principles of simplicity in design, ensuring that your logo is easily recognizable across various platforms and applications.

2.1.2 Incorporating Culinary Themes

Your logo should embody your culinary theme. We explore creative ways to incorporate culinary elements into your logo, whether it's through iconic symbols, stylized utensils, or representations of your signature dishes.

2.2 The Role of Packaging in Branding

2.2.1 Functionality and Aesthetics
Packaging is not just functional; it's a canvas for your brand identity. We discuss the balance between functionality and aesthetics, ensuring that your packaging not only protects your food but also communicates your brand story.

2.2.2 Sustainable Packaging Practices
Sustainability is a growing concern among consumers. We explore sustainable packaging practices, from eco-friendly materials to innovative designs that reduce waste and align with environmentally conscious values.

2.3 Branding Through Visual Consistency

2.3.1 Consistency Across Platforms
Visual consistency builds brand recognition. We explore strategies for maintaining a cohesive visual identity across various platforms, from your website and social media to physical packaging and promotional materials.

2.3.2 Packaging as a Marketing Tool
Packaging is an extension of your marketing strategy. We discuss how well-designed packaging can serve as a marketing tool, influencing customer perception, and encouraging social media sharing.

Section 3: Building a Cohesive Brand Narrative
A brand narrative is the story you tell, and in the culinary world, it's the aroma, taste, and experience you share. This

section explores the art of crafting a cohesive brand narrative that resonates with your audience.

3.1 Storytelling for Emotional Connection

3.1.1 The Power of Culinary Storytelling
Culinary storytelling engages the senses and emotions. We discuss the elements of effective storytelling, from sharing the inspiration behind your dishes to highlighting the journey of your culinary creations.

3.1.2 Humanizing Your Brand
People connect with people. We explore strategies for humanizing your brand, introducing the faces behind the kitchen, and sharing authentic stories that forge a personal connection with your audience.

3.2 Consistency in Brand Communication

3.2.1 Voice and Tone
Consistency in brand communication involves maintaining a consistent voice and tone. We explore how to define your brand's voice, ensuring that the way you communicate aligns with your personality and resonates with your audience.

3.2.2 Multichannel Branding
Your brand narrative should transcend platforms. We discuss the importance of multichannel branding, ensuring that your story is seamlessly woven into your website, social media, marketing materials, and even customer interactions.

3.3 Leveraging Culinary Events and Collaborations

3.3.1 Hosting Culinary Events
Culinary events provide a tangible experience of your brand. We explore the possibilities of hosting events, whether virtual or physical, to showcase your culinary expertise, engage with your audience, and reinforce your brand narrative.

3.3.2 Collaborating with Influencers and Partners
Collaborations amplify your brand reach. We discuss strategies for collaborating with influencers, other businesses, and community partners to extend your brand narrative and tap into new audiences.

Section 4: Conclusion
Creating a stellar brand for your cloud kitchen involves a meticulous blend of identity development, visual design, and narrative crafting. By defining a unique brand personality, designing eye-catching logos and packaging, and weaving a cohesive brand narrative, you establish a brand that not only attracts customers but also fosters loyalty and advocacy.

In the subsequent chapters, we will explore additional dimensions of cloud kitchen management, including customer retention strategies, operational excellence, and the pursuit of culinary innovation. As you embark on the journey of brand creation for your cloud kitchen, let the principles outlined in this chapter guide you toward a future where your brand becomes synonymous with culinary excellence and customer delight.

Cloud Kitchens Unveiled

Chapter 7: Customer Retention Strategies

In the world of cloud kitchens, customer retention is a cornerstone of sustained success. This chapter delves into the art and science of retaining customers, exploring strategies such as loyalty programs, feedback analysis, and personalized experiences that foster lasting relationships.

Section 1: Implementing Loyalty Programs and Discounts

Loyalty programs and discounts are powerful tools for encouraging repeat business and cultivating a dedicated customer base. This section explores the implementation of effective loyalty programs and discount strategies to enhance customer retention.

1.1 Designing a Rewarding Loyalty Program

1.1.1 Understanding Customer Preferences

A successful loyalty program begins with understanding what your customers value. We explore methods for gathering insights into customer preferences, enabling you to tailor rewards that resonate with your audience.

1.1.2 Tiered Loyalty Structures

Tiered loyalty structures provide a sense of progression for customers. We discuss the design principles behind tiered loyalty programs, offering increasingly attractive rewards to customers as they ascend through loyalty tiers.

1.2 Leveraging Discounts Strategically

1.2.1 Timing and Occasion-Based Discounts
Strategic timing of discounts can drive customer engagement. We explore the impact of occasion-based discounts, from seasonal promotions to special events, and how they can be used to boost sales and retention.

1.2.2 Personalized Discount Offers
Personalization adds a personalized touch to your discounts. We discuss the benefits of tailoring discount offers based on customer behavior, preferences, and order history to enhance the effectiveness of your promotional efforts.

1.3 Ensuring Profitability in Loyalty Programs

1.3.1 Cost-Benefit Analysis
Loyalty programs should be profitable for your business. We explore the importance of conducting a cost-benefit analysis, ensuring that the rewards offered align with customer retention goals without compromising profitability.

1.3.2 Analytics for Loyalty Program Optimization
Loyalty programs can be developed on basis of data analytics. We discuss how analytics can be used to track the performance of loyalty initiatives, identify trends, and refine the program for maximum effectiveness.

Section 2: Gathering and Analyzing Customer Feedback

Customer feedback is a goldmine of insights that can guide improvements, enhance customer satisfaction, and inform strategic decisions. This section explores the art of gathering and analyzing customer feedback effectively.

2.1 Establishing Feedback Channels

2.1.1 Surveys and Feedback Forms
Structured surveys and feedback forms provide valuable quantitative data. We explore the design and implementation of surveys, ensuring that the questions asked yield actionable insights to improve your cloud kitchen operations.

2.1.2 Social Media Listening
Social media is a dynamic platform for customer feedback. We discuss the art of social media listening, monitoring customer conversations, and extracting insights that can inform real-time adjustments to your cloud kitchen strategy.

2.2 Encouraging Honest Feedback

2.2.1 Creating a Feedback-Friendly Culture
Customers are more likely to provide feedback in a welcoming environment. We explore strategies for creating a feedback-friendly culture, where customers feel comfortable sharing their opinions and experiences.

2.2.2 Incentivizing Feedback
Incentives can motivate customers to provide feedback. We discuss creative ways to incentivize feedback, whether

through discounts on future orders, exclusive promotions, or participation in contests that engage your customer base.

2.3 Analyzing and Implementing Feedback

2.3.1 Categorizing and Prioritizing Feedback
Not all feedback holds the same weight. We explore methods for categorizing and prioritizing feedback, focusing on addressing issues that have the most significant impact on customer satisfaction and retention.

2.3.2 Closed-Loop Feedback Systems
Closed-loop feedback systems involve closing the feedback loop with customers. We discuss the importance of acknowledging and responding to customer feedback, demonstrating a commitment to continuous improvement and customer satisfaction.

Section 3: Personalizing the Customer Experience

Personalization goes beyond addressing customers by name; it involves tailoring every interaction to their preferences and behaviors. This section explores strategies for personalizing the customer experience in a cloud kitchen setting.

3.1 Utilizing Customer Data for Personalization

3.1.1 Data Collection and Consent
Effective personalization requires customer data. We discuss the principles of responsible data collection and the

importance of obtaining customer consent, building a foundation of trust for personalized interactions.

3.1.2 Creating Customer Profiles

Customer profiles serve as the basis for personalization. We explore the elements of customer profiles, including order history, preferences, and feedback, enabling your cloud kitchen to create tailored experiences for each customer.

3.2 Customizing Menus and Recommendations

3.2.1 Dynamic Menu Displays

Dynamic menu displays adapt to customer preferences. We discuss the implementation of dynamic menus that showcase personalized recommendations based on customer history, enhancing the likelihood of upsells and cross-sells.

3.2.2 Personalized Promotions and Offers

Tailored promotions and offers add a personal touch to marketing efforts. We explore strategies for personalizing promotions, whether through exclusive discounts, personalized bundles, or targeted campaigns based on customer segments.

3.3 Enhancing Customer Communication

3.3.1 Personalized Communication Channels

Customers have preferences for communication channels. We discuss the importance of offering personalized communication options, from email and SMS to app notifications, ensuring that your messages reach customers through their preferred channels.

3.3.2 Celebrating Milestones and Special Occasions

Recognizing customer milestones and special occasions fosters a sense of celebration. We explore how cloud kitchens can personalize customer interactions by acknowledging birthdays, anniversaries, and other significant moments, building a stronger emotional connection.

Section 4: Conclusion

Customer retention is a dynamic interplay of loyalty programs, feedback analysis, and personalized experiences. By implementing effective loyalty initiatives, leveraging customer feedback for continuous improvement, and personalizing every aspect of the customer experience, cloud kitchens can build lasting relationships with their audience.

In the upcoming chapters, we will explore additional dimensions of cloud kitchen management, from operational excellence and culinary innovation to the role of technology in streamlining operations. As you embark on the journey of customer retention for your cloud kitchen, let the principles outlined in this chapter guide you toward a future where every customer not only returns but becomes a loyal advocate for your culinary brand.

Cloud Kitchens Unveiled

Chapter 8: Operational Excellence

Operational excellence is the backbone of a successful cloud kitchen. This chapter delves into the intricacies of managing inventory and the supply chain, optimizing staff training for efficiency and quality, and implementing sustainable practices that contribute to the long-term success of your cloud kitchen.

Section 1: Managing Inventory and Supply Chain

Efficient management of inventory and the supply chain is critical for maintaining a seamless and cost-effective operation. This section explores strategies for effective inventory management, streamlining the supply chain, and ensuring the availability of fresh and high-quality ingredients.

1.1 Inventory Management Strategies

1.1.1 Real-Time Tracking Systems
Real-time tracking systems provide visibility into inventory levels. We explore the implementation of inventory management software and tools that enable cloud kitchens to monitor ingredient levels, prevent stockouts, and reduce waste.

1.1.2 Demand Forecasting for Order Optimization
Demand forecasting involves predicting order volumes based on historical data and trends. We discuss the importance of accurate demand forecasting in optimizing inventory levels,

preventing overstocking, and ensuring timely replenishment of ingredients.

1.2 Streamlining the Supply Chain

1.2.1 Supplier Relationship Management
Effective relationships with suppliers are crucial. We explore strategies for supplier relationship management, including negotiation techniques, communication practices, and collaborative efforts to enhance the efficiency of the supply chain.

1.2.2 Just-in-Time Inventory Systems
Just-in-time (JIT) inventory systems minimize storage costs and waste. We discuss the principles of JIT inventory management, exploring how cloud kitchens can leverage this approach to maintain optimal inventory levels and reduce carrying costs.

1.3 Ensuring Ingredient Quality and Freshness

1.3.1 Quality Assurance Protocols
Quality assurance protocols are essential for ensuring ingredient quality. We explore the establishment of quality standards, inspection procedures, and quality control measures that contribute to the consistency and excellence of your culinary offerings.

1.3.2 Cold Chain Management for Freshness
Preserving the freshness of ingredients is paramount. We discuss the principles of cold chain management, from sourcing to storage and delivery, ensuring that perishable

items maintain their quality and safety throughout the supply chain.

Section 2: Staff Training for Efficiency and Quality

Well-trained staff is the heartbeat of operational excellence. This section explores the development of comprehensive staff training programs that enhance efficiency, uphold quality standards, and contribute to a positive working environment in your cloud kitchen.

2.1 Structuring Effective Training Programs

2.1.1 Onboarding and Orientation

Effective onboarding sets the tone for employee success. We explore onboarding strategies, including orientation sessions, training materials, and mentorship programs that facilitate the smooth integration of new staff members into your cloud kitchen.

2.1.2 Continuous Training for Skill Development

Learning is an ongoing process. We discuss the importance of continuous training programs that focus on skill development, keeping staff members updated on culinary techniques, customer service practices, and the latest technology in the kitchen.

2.2 Implementing Efficiency Protocols

2.2.1 Standard Operating Procedures (SOPs)

Standard Operating Procedures (SOPs) establish consistency in operations. We explore the creation and implementation of SOPs that detail workflows, quality standards, and safety protocols, ensuring that each staff member adheres to a set of best practices.

2.2.2 Cross-Training for Versatility
Cross-training staff members enhances versatility in the kitchen. We discuss the benefits of cross-training programs, enabling employees to perform multiple roles, fostering a collaborative environment, and ensuring operational continuity during peak times or staff shortages.

2.3 Fostering a Positive Work Culture

2.3.1 Employee Recognition and Rewards
Recognition and rewards motivate staff members. We explore strategies for acknowledging and rewarding exceptional performance, fostering a positive work culture, and reinforcing the importance of each team member's contribution to the success of the cloud kitchen.

2.3.2 Communication and Feedback Channels
Good communication lays the groundwork for fostering a constructive work atmosphere. We discuss the establishment of open communication channels, feedback mechanisms, and forums for staff input, creating a culture of transparency, collaboration, and continuous improvement.

Section 3: Implementing Sustainable Practices
Sustainability is not just a buzzword; it's a strategic imperative for the modern cloud kitchen. This section explores the implementation of sustainable practices that

contribute to environmental responsibility, cost efficiency, and the positive perception of your cloud kitchen.

3.1 Sustainable Sourcing of Ingredients

3.1.1 Locally Sourced and Seasonal Ingredients
Locally sourced and seasonal ingredients align with sustainability goals. We discuss the benefits of prioritizing local and seasonal sourcing, supporting regional farmers, reducing carbon footprints, and offering fresh, environmentally conscious menu options.

3.1.2 Certifications and Eco-Friendly Labels
Certifications and eco-friendly labels enhance your brand's credibility. We explore the process of obtaining certifications such as organic or Fair Trade, and how eco-friendly labels communicate your commitment to sustainability to environmentally conscious consumers.

3.2 Waste Reduction and Recycling Initiatives

3.2.1 Comprehensive Waste Audits
Waste audits identify areas for improvement. We explore the conduct of comprehensive waste audits, analyzing kitchen processes to minimize food waste, optimize packaging, and implement recycling initiatives that align with sustainability goals.

3.2.2 Upcycling and Repurposing
Upcycling transforms waste into valuable resources. We discuss creative ways to upcycle and repurpose kitchen waste, such as turning vegetable scraps into compost or using

surplus ingredients in innovative menu specials, minimizing waste and maximizing efficiency.

3.3 Energy Efficiency in Kitchen Operations

3.3.1 Energy-Efficient Appliances and Practices
Energy-efficient appliances and practices contribute to cost savings and environmental conservation. We explore the selection of energy-efficient kitchen equipment, as well as operational practices that minimize energy consumption without compromising output.

3.3.2 Employee Education on Sustainable Practices
Employee awareness is crucial for sustainable operations. We discuss training programs that educate staff members on the importance of sustainable practices, empowering them to contribute to energy efficiency, waste reduction, and environmentally responsible behavior in the kitchen.

Section 4: Conclusion
Operational excellence in a cloud kitchen involves the seamless management of inventory, effective staff training, and the implementation of sustainable practices. By optimizing supply chain processes, investing in comprehensive staff development, and committing to sustainability, your cloud kitchen can not only meet operational challenges but also thrive in an increasingly competitive landscape.

In the forthcoming chapters, we will explore additional dimensions of cloud kitchen management, including the integration of technology for enhanced efficiency, strategies for culinary innovation, and the nuances of marketing in the digital age. As you embark on the journey of operational excellence for your cloud kitchen, let the principles outlined in this chapter guide you toward a future where efficiency, quality, and sustainability define the essence of your culinary operation.

Chapter 9: Financial Management

Financial management is the cornerstone of a successful cloud kitchen operation. This chapter delves into the intricacies of budgeting and forecasting, pricing strategies for profitability, and the art of managing costs while maximizing revenue to ensure the financial health and sustainability of your cloud kitchen.

Section 1: Budgeting and Forecasting for Cloud Kitchens

Effective financial planning starts with the establishment of strong budgeting frameworks and accurate forecasting methodologies. This section explores the methodologies and strategies for creating realistic budgets, accurate financial forecasts, and adapting to dynamic market conditions.

1.1 Creating a Comprehensive Budget

1.1.1 Identifying Fixed and Variable Costs
A comprehensive budget distinguishes between fixed and variable costs. We explore how to identify and categorize various expenses, from rent and utilities to ingredient costs and marketing expenditures, providing a clear overview of your cloud kitchen's financial landscape.

1.1.2 Allocating Resources for Growth
Budgets should align with growth objectives. We discuss strategies for allocating resources strategically, whether for expanding to new locations, investing in technology

upgrades, or launching marketing campaigns to increase brand visibility and customer reach.

1.2 Accurate Financial Forecasting

1.2.1 Utilizing Historical Data for Projections
Historical data provides the basis for precise forecasting. We explore the utilization of historical sales data, customer trends, and market performance to make informed projections and anticipate financial outcomes in different scenarios.

1.2.2 Incorporating Market Trends and Seasonality
Market trends and seasonality impact financial performance. We discuss how to factor in external influences, such as changing consumer preferences and seasonal variations, to create dynamic financial forecasts that adapt to the evolving landscape.

1.3 Adapting to Dynamic Market Conditions

1.3.1 Scenario Planning for Contingencies
Contingency planning is integral to financial resilience. We explore the principles of scenario planning, enabling your cloud kitchen to anticipate and prepare for various scenarios, from economic downturns to unexpected market shifts.

1.3.2 Flexibility in Budget Adjustments
Flexibility is key to adapting to market dynamics. We discuss how to build flexibility into your budget, allowing for adjustments in real-time based on emerging trends,

customer feedback, and the overall performance of your cloud kitchen.

Section 2: Pricing Strategies for Profitability

Setting the right prices is a delicate balance between profitability and customer value. This section explores pricing strategies that maximize revenue while ensuring competitive pricing in the dynamic landscape of the cloud kitchen market.

2.1 Cost-Plus Pricing Models

2.1.1 Calculating Cost of Goods Sold (COGS)

Cost-Plus pricing models start with a clear understanding of COGS. We explore methods for accurately calculating the cost of goods sold, factoring in direct costs associated with producing each menu item, and determining the baseline for pricing decisions.

2.1.2 Establishing Profit Margins

Profit margins define the profitability of each sale. We discuss how to establish profit margins that cover operational costs, contribute to overall financial health, and align with industry standards while remaining attractive to customers.

2.2 Competitive Pricing Strategies

2.2.1 Analyzing Competitor Pricing

Competitor analysis informs pricing decisions. We explore strategies for analyzing competitor pricing, identifying pricing gaps, and positioning your cloud kitchen competitively without compromising on profitability.

2.2.2 Value-Based Pricing
Value-based pricing revolves around perceived value. We discuss the principles of value-based pricing, where the price reflects the perceived value of your culinary offerings, allowing you to capture a share of the market based on the unique value you provide.

2.3 Dynamic Pricing in a Digital Landscape

2.3.1 Utilizing Technology for Dynamic Pricing
Technology enables dynamic pricing adjustments. We explore the integration of technology solutions, such as algorithmic pricing tools and real-time analytics, to implement dynamic pricing strategies that respond to demand fluctuations and market trends.

2.3.2 Promotions and Discounts for Strategic Pricing
Strategic promotions and discounts can influence customer behavior. We discuss how to leverage promotions and discounts strategically, whether to drive sales during off-peak hours, launch new menu items, or reward loyal customers, while maintaining overall pricing integrity.

Section 3: Managing Costs and Maximizing Revenue
Efficient cost management and revenue maximization are the pillars of financial success. This section explores strategies for identifying and controlling costs, optimizing revenue streams, and achieving a healthy balance between income and expenditure.

3.1 Cost Management Strategies

3.1.1 Identifying Cost Drivers
Understanding cost drivers is essential for effective management. We explore how to identify key cost drivers in your cloud kitchen, from labor and ingredient costs to overhead expenses, allowing you to implement targeted cost-saving measures.

3.1.2 Implementing Cost-Reduction Initiatives
Cost-reduction initiatives contribute to overall financial efficiency. We discuss practical strategies for implementing cost-saving measures, whether through renegotiating supplier contracts, optimizing kitchen workflows, or investing in energy-efficient equipment.

3.2 Revenue Optimization Techniques

3.2.1 Diversifying Revenue Streams
Diversification minimizes dependence on a single revenue source. We explore the benefits of diversifying revenue streams, whether through collaborations, catering services, or exclusive partnerships, creating multiple channels for income generation.

3.2.2 Menu Engineering for Profitability
Menu engineering involves optimizing menu items for profitability. We discuss techniques for menu analysis, identifying high-margin items, strategically pricing dishes, and promoting items that contribute most significantly to overall revenue.

3.3 Data-Driven Decision-Making

3.3.1 Utilizing Analytics for Financial Insights
Data analytics provides actionable financial insights. We explore the role of analytics in financial decision-making, from tracking sales performance to identifying trends and opportunities that inform strategic financial planning.

3.3.2 Customer Relationship Management (CRM) for Retention and Revenue
Effective CRM contributes to customer retention and revenue growth. We discuss the integration of CRM systems, leveraging customer data to tailor marketing efforts, identify upsell opportunities, and foster long-term relationships that contribute to sustained revenue.

Section 4: Conclusion

Financial management is the lifeblood of a thriving cloud kitchen. By mastering budgeting and forecasting, implementing pricing strategies for profitability, and effectively managing costs while maximizing revenue, your cloud kitchen can navigate the complexities of the culinary landscape with financial resilience and sustainable growth.

In the upcoming chapters, we will explore additional dimensions of cloud kitchen management, including the integration of technology for enhanced efficiency, strategies for operational excellence, and the nuances of marketing in the digital age. As you embark on the journey of financial management for your cloud kitchen, let the principles outlined in this chapter guide you toward a future where financial success becomes synonymous with your culinary brand.

Chapter 10: Scaling Your Culinary Empire

Scaling your culinary empire is a multifaceted journey that involves replicating success in new locations, exploring franchise and partnership opportunities, and staying innovative to outpace the competition. This chapter provides a comprehensive guide to navigating the challenges and seizing the opportunities that come with expanding your cloud kitchen into a culinary empire.

Section 1: Replicating Success in New Locations
Expanding your cloud kitchen to new locations requires a strategic approach to ensure that the success achieved in one place is replicated elsewhere. This section explores key strategies for maintaining consistency, adapting to local nuances, and thriving in diverse markets.

1.1 Market Analysis and Selection

1.1.1 Identifying Target Demographics
Grasping the demographics of your target audience is indispensable. We delve into the importance of market analysis, helping you identify locations where your culinary offerings align with the preferences and lifestyles of potential customers.

1.1.2 Evaluating Regulatory Landscape
Navigating the regulatory landscape is crucial for a smooth expansion. We discuss the significance of evaluating local regulations, health codes, and licensing requirements to

ensure compliance and mitigate potential challenges in new locations.

1.2 Adapting Your Menu for Local Palates

1.2.1 Tailoring Culinary Offerings
Adapting your menu to local palates is key to acceptance. We explore strategies for tailoring your culinary offerings, incorporating local flavors, and ensuring that your menu resonates with the unique tastes of each community.

1.2.2 Balancing Consistency and Adaptation
Maintaining consistency while adapting to local preferences is a delicate balance. We discuss how to strike this balance, ensuring that your brand retains its identity while also catering to the specific tastes of diverse markets.

1.3 Marketing Strategies for New Locations

1.3.1 Localized Marketing Campaigns
Localized marketing campaigns enhance visibility. We explore the importance of tailoring your marketing strategies to each new location, utilizing local influencers, community events, and geographically targeted advertising to build awareness and attract customers.

1.3.2 Leveraging Customer Feedback from Existing Locations
Feedback from existing locations can inform strategies for new ones. We discuss how to leverage customer feedback from established kitchens, using insights to refine your

offerings, customer service approach, and marketing messages in new locations.

1.4 Operational Replication and Efficiency

1.4.1 Standardizing Operational Processes
Standardized operational processes streamline replication. We explore the importance of creating standardized procedures, from kitchen workflows to order fulfillment and customer service, ensuring efficiency and consistency across multiple locations.

1.4.2 Scalable Technology Solutions
Technology is a catalyst for operational scalability. We discuss the integration of scalable technology solutions, such as order management systems and inventory tracking tools, to facilitate seamless operations as you expand your culinary empire.

Section 2: Exploring Franchise and Partnership Opportunities
Scaling your culinary empire involves not just expanding geographically but also exploring strategic partnerships and franchise opportunities. This section delves into the intricacies of these endeavors, offering insights into their benefits, challenges, and effective implementation.

2.1 Franchising as a Growth Strategy

2.1.1 Building a Franchise Model
A well-structured franchise model is the foundation of successful franchising. We explore the key components of

building a franchise model, from defining territories and fees to outlining support structures for franchisees.

2.1.2 Selecting Franchisees and Establishing Partnerships

Choosing the right franchisees is critical. We discuss criteria for selecting franchise partners, evaluating their alignment with your brand values, financial stability, and dedication to maintaining the standards of your cloud kitchen.

2.2 Partnership Strategies for Expansion

2.2.1 Collaborating with Established Brands

Strategic collaborations can expedite expansion. We explore the benefits of partnering with established brands, whether in the food industry or other sectors, to tap into new customer bases, cross-promote offerings, and create mutually beneficial relationships.

2.2.2 Joint Ventures and Shared Ventures

Joint ventures and shared ventures can diversify your growth strategies. We discuss the intricacies of forming partnerships where resources, risks, and rewards are shared, providing a collaborative approach to scaling your culinary empire.

2.3 International Expansion Considerations

2.3.1 Adapting to Global Culinary Trends

Expanding internationally requires a nuanced approach. We explore how to adapt your culinary offerings to global trends, respecting local culinary traditions while infusing your brand with a universally appealing and innovative flair.

2.3.2 Navigating Cultural Sensitivities

Cultural sensitivity is paramount in international expansion. We discuss strategies for navigating cultural nuances, respecting local customs, and fostering a positive brand perception that resonates with diverse global audiences.

Section 3: Be innovative and overcome competition

Innovation is the key to sustained success and staying ahead of the competition. This section explores strategies for fostering a culture of innovation, adopting emerging technologies, and continuously evolving your culinary offerings to captivate customers.

3.1 Cultivating a Culture of Innovation

3.1.1 Encouraging Creativity Within Your Team

Innovation starts from within. We discuss strategies for fostering a culture of creativity and innovation within your team, encouraging employees to contribute ideas, experiment with new flavors, and actively participate in the evolution of your culinary offerings.

3.1.2 Implementing Idea Generation Platforms

Dedicated platforms for idea generation can fuel innovation. We explore the implementation of systems that collect and assess ideas from team members, customers, and industry trends, providing a structured approach to innovation.

3.2 Embracing Technology for Culinary Innovation

3.2.1 Integration of Smart Kitchen Technologies
Smart kitchen technologies enhance efficiency and innovation. We explore the integration of technologies such as IoT devices, automation, and AI-driven tools, transforming your kitchen into a hub of culinary innovation and operational excellence.

3.2.2 Data-Driven Menu Development
Data analytics informs menu development. We discuss how to leverage customer data, feedback, and market trends to make data-driven decisions about your menu, ensuring that it remains relevant, appealing, and ahead of the competition.

3.3 Continuous Learning and Adaptation

3.3.1 Monitoring Industry Trends and Customer Preferences
Staying ahead requires vigilance. We explore the importance of continuous learning, monitoring industry trends, and staying attuned to shifting customer preferences, enabling your culinary empire to adapt proactively to changes in the market landscape.

3.3.2 Learning from Successes and Failures
Both successes and failures provide valuable lessons. We discuss the significance of analyzing the outcomes of new initiatives, learning from what works and what doesn't, and applying these insights to refine your strategies for ongoing success.

Section 4: Conclusion

Scaling your culinary empire is a dynamic and multifaceted journey that requires a combination of strategic planning, adaptability, and a commitment to innovation. By replicating success in new locations, exploring franchise and partnership opportunities, and staying innovative, your cloud kitchen can not only expand its footprint but also establish itself as a trailblazer in the ever-evolving culinary landscape.

In the final chapters, we will explore additional dimensions of cloud kitchen management, including strategies for customer retention, building a compelling brand, and achieving operational excellence. As you embark on the journey of scaling your culinary empire, let the principles outlined in this chapter guide you toward a future where your brand becomes synonymous with culinary excellence and innovation.

Conclusion: Building and Sustaining a Thriving Cloud Kitchen

As we conclude this comprehensive guide on establishing and operating a successful cloud kitchen, it's imperative to reflect on the key principles that underpin culinary excellence and sustainable growth in the modern gastronomic landscape. The journey from conceptualizing your cloud kitchen to scaling it into a culinary empire is a dynamic and challenging endeavor, requiring a nuanced understanding of various facets of the industry. Let's encapsulate the essence of our exploration and offer a closing statement that resonates with the aspiring cloud kitchen entrepreneur.

Culmination of Culinary Expertise

Throughout this book, we've delved into the intricacies of crafting a culinary concept that not only aligns with your passion but also resonates with your target audience. Identifying your niche, developing a menu that tantalizes taste buds, and leveraging data for continuous menu optimization are the foundational steps toward culinary excellence.

The Art of Operational Finesse

Operational excellence forms the backbone of a thriving cloud kitchen. From choosing the right location and designing an efficient kitchen layout to complying with regulations and embracing technology for streamlined operations, we've navigated the operational intricacies that contribute to a seamless and efficient kitchen environment.

Financial Mastery for Long-Term Success

In the realm of cloud kitchens, financial management is the linchpin that ensures sustained success. From budgeting and forecasting to implementing pricing strategies and managing costs, we've explored the financial intricacies that empower your cloud kitchen to navigate the economic landscape with resilience and foresight.

Customer-Centric Strategies

Customer retention is not merely a metric; it's the heartbeat of a flourishing cloud kitchen. Loyalty programs, feedback analysis, personalized experiences, and effective communication channels are the cornerstones of strategies designed to not only attract but retain a dedicated customer base.

Crafting a Compelling Brand Identity

Beyond the culinary creations, your brand is a narrative—a story that resonates with customers. From developing a unique brand identity to designing eye-catching logos and packaging, we've explored the principles that elevate your cloud kitchen from a place to order food to a brand synonymous with culinary excellence.

Scaling Strategies for Culinary Empires

As you embark on the journey of scaling your culinary empire, replicating success in new locations, exploring franchise and partnership opportunities, and staying innovative are the strategic imperatives that will define the trajectory of your brand in the competitive culinary landscape.

A Vision for the Future

In closing, envision your cloud kitchen not merely as a culinary venture but as a transformative force in the gastronomic world. Embrace the challenges as opportunities, innovate relentlessly, and let the principles outlined in this guide be the compass guiding you toward a future where your cloud kitchen stands as a testament to culinary artistry, operational finesse, and unwavering customer loyalty.

May your journey be marked by the sizzle of success, the aroma of innovation, and the satisfaction of a well-crafted culinary experience. As you embark on this gastronomic adventure, remember that the heart of every cloud kitchen beats with the passion to deliver not just meals, but memorable moments that linger on the palates and in the hearts of your valued patrons.

Here's to the culinary empire you're destined to build—one delectable dish, one satisfied customer, and one thriving kitchen at a time. Bon appétit!

About the Author:

Raj Dev Acharya is not just an entrepreneur; he is a visionary leader with a rich tapestry of experience spanning over 30 years. His journey in the business world has been shaped by an unwavering passion for innovation, a commitment to personal growth, and an innate ability to navigate the complexities of the entrepreneurial landscape.

A Legacy of Leadership:
At the core of Raj Dev Acharya's success is a set of guiding principles—honor, realism, perseverance, and patience. These values have not only defined his personal journey but have also become the pillars of his leadership philosophy. With an acute focus on developing a foundation of strength, strategy, and excellence, Raj has cultivated a legacy of leadership that extends beyond the boardroom.

Investing in Others:
One of Raj's distinctive qualities is his belief in the power of investing in others. He is not just a leader; he is a mentor who is passionate about unlocking the full potential of those around him. His leadership style is characterized by a blend of domain expertise, analytical thinking, and creative problem-solving, creating an environment where individuals thrive and contribute their best.

Purpose-Driven Commitment:
Raj's commitment to purpose is unwavering. Whether navigating through challenges, closing deals, or inspiring teams, he embodies a relentless pursuit of purpose-driven

success. His financial acumen, combined with an ability to pitch and close deals, positions him as a valuable asset in the entrepreneurial arena.

Mastering Relationships and Communication:
A master at building and managing relationships, Raj excels in the art of effective communication. His ability to inspire and motivate teams is not just a skill but a testament to his leadership ethos. With a broad perspective on the bigger picture, he navigates both macro and micromanagement effortlessly, leveraging industry trends to drive success.

A Holistic Approach to Business:
Raj seamlessly integrates all facets of business, including personnel, economic landscapes, governmental regulations, market dynamics, clientele, workforce, technological innovations, and business partnerships. His collaborative approach and strong ethical compass create a harmonious and thriving enterprise, reflecting a deep understanding of the interconnected nature of modern business ecosystems.

Seeking New Horizons:
In his constant pursuit of new opportunities and challenges, Raj Dev Acharya remains an open-minded and forward-thinking entrepreneur. His invitation to explore the world of opportunities together is not just an offer but a call to elevate the game of entrepreneurship to new heights. Raj is a bridge-builder, connecting with like-minded entrepreneurs to collectively shape the future of business.

As you embark on the journey through this book, remember that the insights and guidance within these pages are not just theoretical—they are the product of real-world experience, leadership, and a passion for creating a meaningful impact. Raj Dev Acharya's legacy is not just a story; it's an invitation to join him in the pursuit of excellence, innovation, and the boundless possibilities that entrepreneurship offers.

A Personal Invitation to Explore the World of Cloud Kitchens

Dear Esteemed Readers,

I trust this correspondence finds you in robust health and buoyant spirits. It is with immense pleasure and anticipation that I extend my warmest greetings to each of you.

I am writing to you not just as the author of this book, but as a fellow entrepreneur, a visionary, and someone deeply passionate about the ever-evolving landscape of the culinary world. This book, " **Cloud Kitchens Unveiled: An All-Encompassing Manual for Initiating and Expanding Your Culinary Dominion**," has been a labor of love—a culmination of my experiences, insights, and the invaluable lessons learned over a journey that spans more than three decades.

In these pages, you will find not just a guide to setting up and running a cloud kitchen but a roadmap infused with the essence of innovation, operational finesse, and the artistry of creating culinary experiences that resonate with the modern consumer.

Why a book on cloud kitchens, you might ask? The answer lies in the transformative power of this culinary concept. Cloud kitchens are more than just a trend; they represent a paradigm shift in how we approach food, business, and the intersection of technology and gastronomy. It is a realm where creativity meets efficiency, where traditional boundaries are redefined, and where opportunities for growth abound.

As you navigate through the chapters, I invite you to embrace this journey with an open mind and a spirit of exploration. Whether you are a seasoned entrepreneur looking to venture into the culinary world or someone with a passion for food and innovation, this book is designed to be your companion, providing insights, strategies, and a roadmap to success in the dynamic realm of cloud kitchens.

I am a firm believer in the efficacy of shared knowledge and collective progress. It is my sincere hope that the principles outlined in this book serve not only as a guide but as a catalyst for your own culinary odyssey. Let's explore the world of opportunities together, challenge ourselves, and elevate the game of entrepreneurship to new heights.

Your feedback, thoughts, and experiences are not just welcomed; they are an integral part of the ongoing conversation. Feel free to reach out, share your insights, and let's continue to learn and grow together.

I extend my heartfelt appreciation for joining me on this voyage. Here's to the exciting adventure that awaits in the world of cloud kitchens.

Warm regards,

Raj Dev Acharya
Author, " Cloud Kitchens Unveiled: An All-Encompassing Manual for Initiating and Expanding Your Culinary Dominion"

www.ingramcontent.com/pod-product-compliance
Lightning Source LLC
LaVergne TN
LVHW061625070526
838199LV00070B/6577